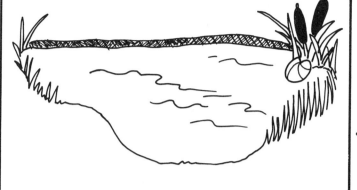

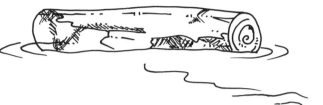

On the back: What did the frog do in the water?

A green frog is on the log.

This is a big pond.

Jump into the water, frog.

A log is in the pond.

On the back: What will Chipper look like now?

"You will like it. Do
not try to get away."

"Isn't this fun, Chipper?
How nice you will look."

"Look out! What a mess
you have made."

"Come here, Chipper.
It is time for your bath."

                                       Read, Think, Cut & Paste

On the back: How did the bone get underground?

What a big bone he found.
Yum, yum, yum.

Sid had a good lunch.
Now he will rest.

Sid began to dig.
Dirt went all over.

Sniff, sniff, sniff. Sid smelled
something good.

       Read, Think, Cut & Paste

On the back: What will turtle and his friends play?

I play with my friends.

I live by a pond.

I duck under the water to eat.

I swim around all day.

4   Read, Think, Cut & Paste

and

On the back:　　　　What will Coco do now?

She sits in a sunny spot
and wags her tail.

She sees a bird go by.

Coco is a happy dog. She has
a big yard to play in.

She runs up the yard after
a butterfly.

On the back: What job can Kiwi do?

Kiwi did not get the job. He went away sad.	"I want a job. I will ask in here," said Kiwi.
"I want a job." "How can a Kiwi help me?" asked Mr. Green.	"I can fix them this way," said Kiwi.

and

On the back: Where has Mr. Panda gone?

"What are you eating,
Mr. Bear?"
"I am NOT a bear!"

"Hello, Mr. Bear."
"I am not a bear."

"Oh! I did not know and now
Mr. Panda has gone away."

"Why are you running away,
Mr. Bear?"
"I'm not a BEAR! I'm a Panda!"

7   Read, Think, Cut & Paste

On the back: What did Mrs. Wig-Wag get?

"Now I can go out and shop,"
said Mrs. Wig-Wag.

"I want to go out, but
I must do my jobs first."

Mrs. Wig-Wag made her
bed fast.

She did dishes fast, too.

8   Read, Think, Cut & Paste

 and

On the back: What will Otto see when he dives?

Now he can eat the clam.

Otto hits the clam with a rock to crack the shell.

Otto likes to swim in the water.

He can dive down to get a clam.

 Read, Think, Cut & Paste

 and

On the back: What did Huggy do at her friend's?

"I will go on a boat."
And she did.

She came to a puddle that was
too deep and too wide to cross.

Littly Huggy Bug was on her
way to visit a friend.

Little Huggy Bug looked around.
"I know what to do," she said.

On the back: How can Bud take care of his teeth?

Now Bud can cut down trees again.

The dentist did fix the tooth.

Bud felt bad. His tooth hurt.

"We will go to the dentist. He will fix it," said Mom.

11   Read, Think, Cut & Paste

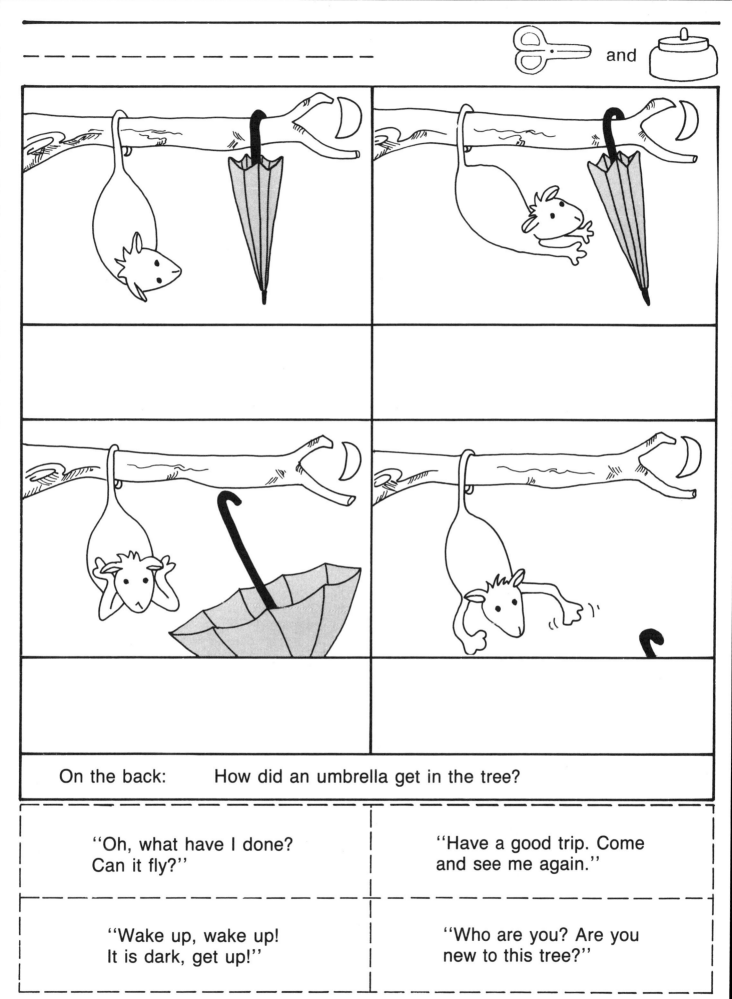

On the back: How did an umbrella get in the tree?

"Oh, what have I done?
Can it fly?"

"Have a good trip. Come
and see me again."

"Wake up, wake up!
It is dark, get up!"

"Who are you? Are you
new to this tree?"

       Read, Think, Cut & Paste

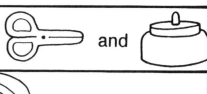

On the back: How did Rabbit paint the flowers?

"How pretty the flowers
look now."

"The eggs are painted and
I have this paint left."

"I know what I will do.
I will paint the flowers."

"Can you help me, Bird?
It is fun."

and

On the back: What tools did the dog use?

On the back: What magic trick do you like best?

"I will do a magic trick for you."

"Two tickets for the magic show, please."

"Oh, look! What a funny trick."

"Can we sit here? I want to see all of the magic show."

     15   Read, Think, Cut & Paste

and

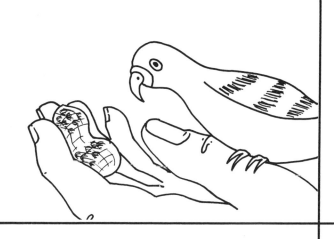

On the back: How did Flash get out of the cage?

"There is Flash on Dad's pipe. Let's catch him!"

"Come here, Flash. Here is something good."

Flash is happy to be back. He is singing.

"Look! Flash is out of his cage."

©1979 by EVAN-MOOR CORP.   16   Read, Think, Cut & Paste

On the back: How can Fish thank his friend?

"Thank-you. You are a good friend."

"See the pretty shells. I wish I had them at my house."

"I can help you, little friend. I have many arms."

"This will take a long time."

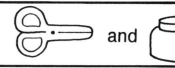 and

On the back: What will they do after lunch?

"It's fun to picnic in the park with friends," laughed Ann.

"What can I do this sunny day?" asked Ann Ant.

"So Ann asks all of her friends to take lunch to the park.

"Ask your friends to go on a picnic," said Mrs. Ant.

©1979 by EVAN-MOOR CORP.   18   Read, Think, Cut & Paste

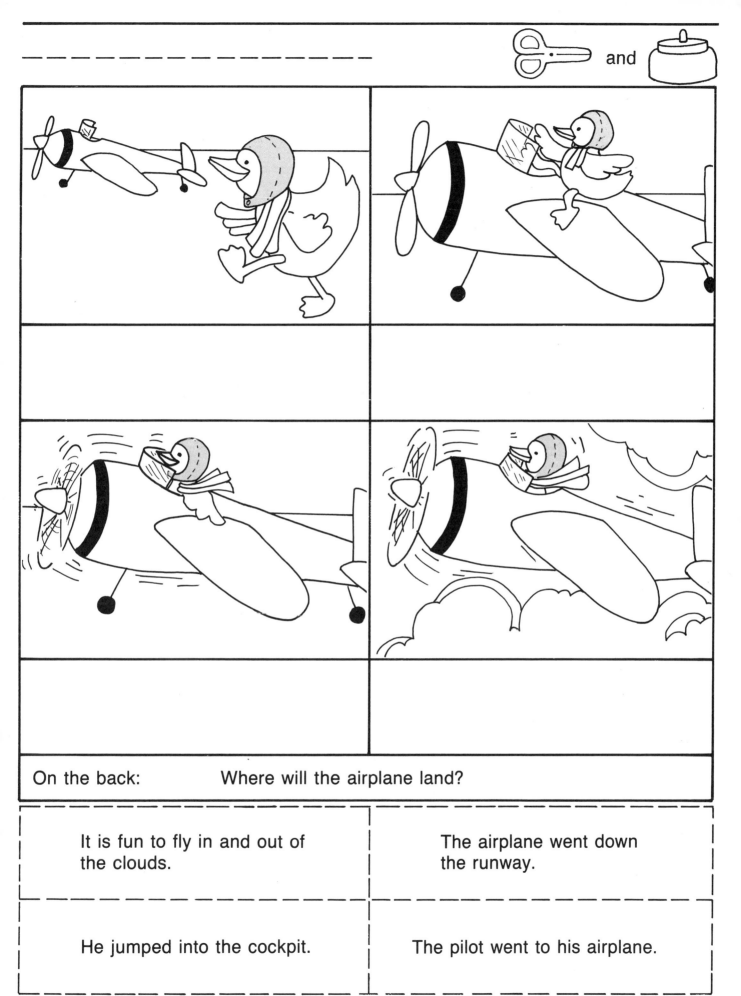

On the back: Where will the airplane land?

It is fun to fly in and out of the clouds.

The airplane went down the runway.

He jumped into the cockpit.

The pilot went to his airplane.

19   Read, Think, Cut & Paste

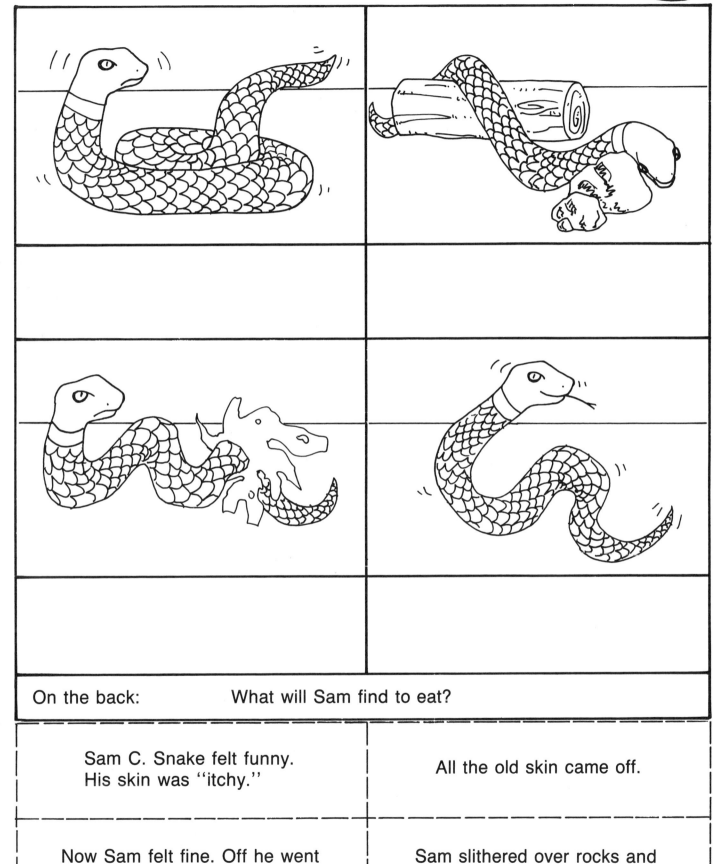

On the back: What will Sam find to eat?

Sam C. Snake felt funny.
His skin was "itchy."

All the old skin came off.

Now Sam felt fine. Off he went
to find something to eat.

Sam slithered over rocks and
under logs.

20   Read, Think, Cut & Paste